Patching Me Together

Poems by
Margaret A. Harrell

Paperback ISBN: 979-8-9860526-7-0

Hardcover ISBN: 979-8-9860526-6-3

A Published in Heaven Series Book

Published in Heaven Books include titles by His Holiness The Dalai Lama,
President Jimmy Carter, Thomas Merton, Seamus Heaney, Hunter S.
Thompson, Jack Kerouac, Andy Warhol, Allen Ginsberg, Yoko Ono, William S.
Burroughs, Edvard Munch, Diane di Prima, Jim Carroll, Amiri Baraka, Gregory
Corso, John Updike, Rita Dove, Wendell Berry, David Amram, Douglas Brinkley,
BONO, Ron Whitehead, Lawrence Ferlinghetti, and many more.

Published in conjunction with Saeculum University Press of Sibiu, Romania,
and Raleigh, North Carolina

For inquiries, signed copies, and speaking requests,
contact marharrell@hotmail.com
margaretharrell.com

Front cover image and design, plus part-title illustration: Grant Goodwine,
grantgoodwine.bigcartel.com/

Back cover bio photograph: Hiltrud Wagner

Interior and back cover design: Deborah Perdue, illuminationgraphics.com

"So what happens to a consciousness" image: Margaret A. Harrell

Contents

Part One

In the Living Room

In the living room the men huddled over cards
Smoke filled the air
Upstairs a little girl lay on the top step of the stairs,
Weighing the odds.
Should she go down?
She was only two and a half.
They might get upset.
They might frown, even spank me,
In front of my daddy's friends.

To go downstairs or not to go downstairs
To face life or not face life
To take risks or play it safe?
Was there any doubt?
How long did she hesitate?

She went down.
Smiles broke over some of the men's faces
As she made her way over to one
He lifted her into his lap
As he had so often lifted her into the front seat beside him
Perched on top of his Fuller Brush Man book of samples
But not in a car this time, in his lap he opened his hand,
Showing her the cards
Spreading them wide so she could see them all

Shhhhhuuuuusss
Not a word, her uncle Hunter said
He wasn't really her uncle
But shuuuush
Here's the cards we're playing with
Now watch while I play the hand.

So She Said

Two people, the psychic innocently said, were king and queen of a tropical island

in the Pacific

centuries ago

They both had second sight

open

They served their people

but suffered because of it

One wanted to come back in this lifetime as a king

The other nevertheless did not want to be queen again

Too much sacrifice, too painful.

"That," she said, "was you and Hunter"

among other lifetimes

as children in India,

girls in the Middle East, who could not talk openly and confided in each other

It explained a lot

that I didn't want to be queen

It hurt

Did not, in modern parlance,

want to be famous

with a large following

The island queen did not want to repeat that history

The island king, he thought it was worth it

Bring it on

Make me king again

And

give us both again

second sight

Well, that part, yes

a peek into the future, into the present

Make us

in a sense

Clairvoyant

So be it.

Time to Make a Composite

I had long been curious about past lives

Who isn't?

Did they really exist?

What were mine?

But I expected daylight-clear memories

no doubt

In fact, the memories were in

side slants

subtle

based in feeling that said, yes, I "remember" that

Time to try to make a composite

Bring myself up to date

Not just the memories of a mere current lifetime

But what I came into it with

Who I was, coming in

Well, just a glimpse

The Nun

Another past life I feel authentically connected to as me

Was a female nun in Tibet

in a monastery hundreds of years ago

I spent my time creating and releasing symbol patterns

fully believing in them

as I sent them out,

these symbols going into the world

I see myself at a window, looking over a vast beautiful expanse of nature

gardens,

leaning out as I put my patterns, my symbols, into

the air, where they fell down into, sailed to meet, crash landed into,
Earth

into the atmosphere in Tibet and on from there

Like Penelope weaving,

consciously

making the symbols

But what is different in that and today,

in light body work,

I do hundreds of years later

The nun looking quite different

I suppose

a face American, not Tibetan

No longer at a monastery window

but the picture the same

as vibrations now

symbolic actions

symbols

transmitted into the world

we all do it

this way is just assigned, organized, focused

Standing in the center of our large self

sending out

"patterns" of who we are

from the one

far and

wide

into wherever

picked up

Twofold

Christ as an individual,

I had initiations with,

it suddenly came to me,

is that and also, of course, a principle

That is—

a point

and

a quantum mirror

a wave

We all are

I suddenly realized

Yes, individuals—

That's the point—but also,

all of us

every one

are waves

and inside waves

the point

That's the me I know

the wave

of ourself, that reaches way beyond our

3-D

Point

Hi, I say, as a point

Hi—the wave picks it up, translates it perhaps into a smile

resonates it around far and wide

Hi, I say

and the world

perhaps

smiles

Wartime

Rilke spent years in silence

His poetry was barricaded where he could not access it

the spigot of writing closed up

The words failed him

It refused to come, no matter how gently he approached

with what desperation he stared at the blank page, pen in hand, ink at his side

Nobody can counsel and help you, nobody. There is only one single way. Go into yourself. Search for the reason that bids you write; find out whether it is spreading out its roots in the deepest places of your heart, acknowledge to yourself whether you would have to die if it were denied you to write.

—Ranier Maria Rilke

I know no advice for you save this: to go into yourself and test the deeps in which your life takes rise; at its source you will find the answer to the question whether you must create. Accept it, just as it sounds, without inquiring into it. Perhaps it will turn out that you are called to be an artist. Then take that destiny upon yourself and bear it, its burden and its greatness, without ever asking what recompense might come from outside. For the creator must be a world for himself and find everything in himself and in Nature to whom he has attached himself.

—Rilke

Is it so today?

Are those days over?

Do we even have the mentality, the experience,

to arrive at this point of view

this depth of our understanding?

    Let not a single one of the cleanly-struck hammers of my heart

    deny me, through a slack, or a doubtful, or

    a broken string.

Skidding to a Halt

1914.

Wartime
Not a drop of ink splashing into a word
for ten years.
his property confiscated, millions facing death

But then
something pealed apart the closed edges
of Creation
It peeped its head out

after a decade of war
the closed-up well opened wide
a volcano hidden beneath
Duino Elegies
he raced to keep up
the repressed lines that had hidden, refusing to
contradict the horror of the war with poetic depths till
they were deep enough
they spurted out

immortal poetry

well worth

the wait

Marooned in Germany, blocked from his Paris home

his property taken away

It was a minor loss with all the bodies dying

Then conscripted as a soldier

Good Lord

Then the poet

transferred to a desk,

blocked

emptied out

till the deluge

rescued the

Duino Elegies

As, on their own, they, powered by his commitment to them

translated the wartime suffering

into stanzas

Finally in Switzerland in 1922, finishing them up and

also here came

Sonnets to Orpheus

Charmed by Australian violinist Alma Moodie

"What a sound, what richness, what determination. That and the *Sonnets to Orpheus*, those were two strings of the same voice. And she plays mostly Bach!" he said.

Bach, good Lord,
thinking of the little girl at the piano at seven, myself
forgetting the Bach recital piece
Going upwards mentally, inwards,
or just lifted outside mind
into who knows what ethers of collective energy
Overarching
to come down with a Life Plan
A module of it
A capsule of Beginning-
End.

Is it possible I too have been silenced

Self-silenced

And this is the

End of it

the

Outpouring

Sonnets to Life

minus the fourteen lines,

the iambic pentameter

Past and

Present

Always present

Pastpresentfuture

In the Here and Now

Part Two

1990s

Je suis *l'alpha-omega*.
Tu es *le contenu*.

—Ion Mircea

Earnestly, he looked at me as he said it, in French:

"I am the alpha-omega. You are the content."

Beginning-end

the male

in charge, doing the job, getting there

BUT

Along the way it fills up with

content

Does not just shoot for the end,

in a wide arc, a touchdown pass

The End arrives satisfied

fulfilled

Beginning having

brought to the End

—*telling me male to female*—

le contenu

Now that history has to be seen in terms of spacetime, what does that do to the Alpha-Omega principle?

How, if all time is present in itself—if it in fact observes not the divisions of night/day/months/years/centuries, if those are not the way it conducts itself—does this principle speak to us today?

No one thought to

say—jumping up from discovering phase space, spacetime and

nonlinearity—Wait a minute. Hold it.

What does this mean, in terms

of

the Beginning and the End

that we used to think of as linear (a–z) called Alpha

OMEGA; is it still linear; is it string? or what does

this mean?

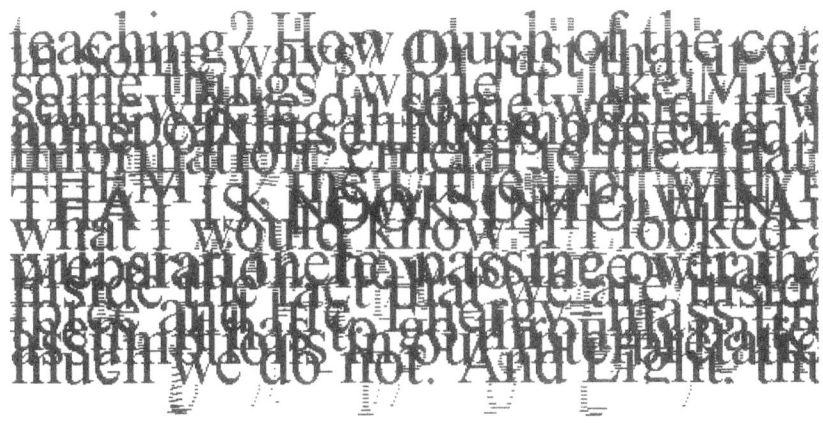

So What Happens to a Consciousness When We Don't Get the Story Straight?

When we curtain the teaching? How much of the consciousness do we lose?

I discovered that in my own self were bits of information crucial to me that if extended would imply shifts in current thinking. Why not extend them?

I, the Little Dot, with no extension in my human, or personality, self, yet did have the awareness that I knew something. These many years hence am at the stage where

I can look into them.

That is, look into what was being carried—from where and containing what? I can study what I would know if I looked and opened the tube or capsule.

Part Three

Being Brought into Existence by You

This is how I now saw you. This evening. These last days. The new period.

Perhaps in my birth, and this is indeed my birth, getting into your vibration.

As you send it. You birth me. You send me the song that is your frequency.

Letting me radiate it, you show me that I am being born in you.
OR out of
You. Or as or through.

All the words relationally attempting to explain.
Yet what I am is this vibration that
you turn me into. That I hold.
That I do not question or waver from. That I wonder, though I do not,
how long—if forever—I will hold it thus.
Or that it is something so intensely
extraordinary, it is the peak of my life. It is as I unite with you.
Who is who?

That is, as I go forward in time,

In the exact trajectory of this specific moment

If uninterfered with, is it me?—me

there at the end of the movement?

Or at what exact moment does it turn into

someone or something

else?

Thus, I believe the invention of the Alpha-Omega

How Jesus came to invent himself

And there must be some reason I am learning this now

Something that has changed

That wants rectification

And immortalization. Some reason that it came to me now.

OR DID I COME TO REMEMBER?

Yet is this not true that in spite of the invisibility of that moment,

Now, it is actually that you are here, remembering and still present, showing me

this even as you remember

Showing me that this was the extension of that, present then

If one could see time as one dimension

But also then, the symbols around a moment help take it into its physical features

That might have been forgotten. But this is not that.

This is remembered, again-present feelings. But they are yours, and they are

in the past, but they have been picked up, or I can see the rims around that day

And those rims are time's. Time's circles that notch the years. I could not see

in multiple rims.

Now I can.

Energized, not just imagined and projected as form without energy of presence.

These are holomovement pieces, functioning in that way in a way

of projections. But if not, are multiply formed, multiply present, living memories.

Stopped in whatever time rims they move through, one after the other in a motif

that is connected.

I had a Cross Unusual

I wore it always around my neck

Until one day it disappeared

But not before you had

I got the cross around your neck

The day they found you dead

One day your cross around my neck

disappeared

Late in the night

You, Dimension

Who could go on forever

And me

Dimension who

Must keep up

Part Four

Point Taken

He wasn't dead
For when they said caps off to him
He did a recap

Took a pass
Realized too late
It was the Vita Pass

It was a cold summer day
When someone who realized she'd bypassed her life
Passed the news to her
Don't you ever get on it
Don't take that turn
Where you find you're on 831
on the Vita
Pass

But what do you do
When you see all roads you're congregating toward are headed to it,
All traffic points that way
That everything, then, must have led up to it
to this impasse

Instead of crashing head on

Squared off after all cars perhaps clinked lights

In the center of the road

Then each turned into its lane

Toward or now arrived at the destination

The Vita Pass

But was it Vita Nuova or Dulce Vita

that was passed

When the turn was what all roads led to

as to Rome

When it was all the traffic in your life that met there

Right and left

As if centered

And took the turn together

BYPASSING WHAT?

When they streamed together

onto 831—

And a voice told you this was it, you were on

THE VITA PASS.

Mistakes Avoided

Coattails latched onto
of the most exciting men I ever me
Latched onto the coattails and risking little
saw every kind of variety there was in the world
Did I say risking little
risking everything
just in my own way
Not duplicating the hell-bent risk-taking
of the coattails I was
Hanging
Onto

Dependency,
I didn't mind it for a while
Not now, of course
But I was young
No,
I didn't mind being dependent on daredevils
for a while
Till I looked
Inside

A Daredevil

Falling in love with a daredevil

Admiration oozing out of the pores

Oh, if I could be like that

Could be such a

Risk-taker

You do it for me

You aren't afraid of death, it appears

And then it rubbed off

Or no, I found alive inside me

Not the passive onlooker with the attraction

But the telescope able to see deep within to where

taking great risks in stride

living life as a depth probe

And a high

It suited me inside

Something in me could navigate it

and come out

On top

God Took Me to the Top of the Mountain

After that I wasn't afraid

Oh, I was afraid

Could be,

of anything

But it was minor

It didn't count

I had a fearless trust

stronger than that

because God took me

to look out from

The top of

The mountain

"Mountain of God,"

He told me.

What?

Well, it depends on how you pronounce your name

Harrell, OK

"in Hebrew

We say Harr-*El*"

Like Hara, I thought,

But he went on

El means God, like Ah

And Harr

Mountain

Harr-

El

Mountain

Of God

That's your name

Acknowledgments

This year I have been blessed and surrounded by the love and care and high spirits of my North Carolina Dance Studio, Raleigh, North Carolina, ballet teachers and the owner, Kerstie Spadie. They have kept my lungs filled and my spirits high, sending me video clips and Zoom dance classes when I had to take a time-out from the studio. It ws incomparable. Far away in Belgium, where I had to cancel a trip, my friends stayed often in my thoughts—Hiltrud, Chris, Mariejke, Frank, and my Brussels women pals, who all mean so much to me. These underlying friendships—the energy they sent me, as did my two sisters and birth family—joined with the wonderful energy of the DaBen & Orin teachings, the energy field, to keep me floating in joy through a difficult health issue, now mostly resolved. I thank the powers that be for trusting I could get through that and it would be a viable path to take me into new positions of consciousness and contribution here on Earth. I am thankful for the spirit energy that wrote with me. And for the books we produced this year, short in length but now four and counting in 2022. At my side for all but this one was Little Hans, my constant companion. Lastly, for contributing the cover and the book design, a huge shout-out to the spectacular painter Grant Goodwine and the gifted interior designer Deborah Perdue.

Praise for Margaret Harrell's Books

Poetry

Particle Piñata Poems

"The time of the grandmothers, of the nurturing healing feminine energy has arrived. Patriarchy has sewn destruction long enough. We must all, female and male, become healers, seers. In her epic PARTICLE PIÑATA, author Margaret Ann Harrell stands in direct lineage with the desert mystics, the poet prophets of old and, simultaneously, with the contemporary cutting edge avant-garde. In a whirling dance with the creative forces of the universe Harrell draws explicit and implicit lines to Rumi, Blake, Yeats, Joyce, Jung, and others while forging mystical connections with clouds and coastlines, dancing in the borderlands of space and time, of being and not being, of embracing and letting go. And she accomplishes it all in her own distinctly original poetic voice. Through decades of carrying these poems from continent to continent, Margaret Ann Harrell has continued to add new poems and photos, to edit and revise, to transform her self into an ever evolving being, into this masterpiece book. I can't recommend it highly enough. Go ahead, open the front cover and enter. You'll never be the same."

—Ron Whitehead, U.S. National Beat Poet Laureate 2020–'22

"The poetry of Margaret Ann Harrell reads like a Zhuangzi of the 21st century, taking its reader through a spiritual Odyssey, where one can hear the cosmic beat in the rhythm of the word play, the pulse of heartfelt mind-blowing experiences revealing a vast span of messages from beyond. It shows the craftmanship of a female shaman who has the power to catch such a dazzling wild and free roaming content into the nets of poems. Here is a biopic in words, a biographical epic, a story of a lifetime full of surprising leaps into the story of Earth and the Cosmic Drama, a rite de passage (read the passage) initiating its reader into multiversal dimensions, bringing meaning to life where few have been looking to find it. This great bold poetry full of wit and spirit reads as a unique treat, a gift from those who know how to sow the seed for what really matters on earth: a choice to live a life guided by love and light. For those who are in love with poetry, share this genuine gift and the sheer joy of it! If you want to, go ahead!"

—Chris Van de Velde (MA Philosophy, lover of wisdom), Belgium

Other Books

The Hell's Angels Letters: Hunter S. Thompson, Margaret Harrell and the Making of an American Classic
(available only at Norfolk Press: norfolkpress.com)

"Thompson's motto might well have been 'Nothing in moderation.' For *The* Hell's Angels *Letters*, Margaret Ann Harrell—in collaboration with Ron Whitehead—has assembled a dossier of all her correspondence with Thompson during the time she worked as the editor of the gonzo writer's 'strange and terrible saga of the outlaw motorcycle gangs.' Typed manuscript pages, scribbled notes, photographs, interviews and all sorts of period ephemera relating to *Hell's Angels* allow the reader a valuable, behind-the-scenes glimpse into the making of this classic of New Journalism."

—Michael Dirda, the *Washington Post*

"As the title implies, this book is mainly comprised of letters between Harrell and Thompson, some typed and some handwritten, and all printed here in color. Of course, there are already two collections of Hunter Thompson's letters available, but somehow they are even more enjoyable when read in the original form. Whether typed or scrawled in giant letters with a red pen, Thompson's correspondence is invariably annotated and corrected in his unique way, adding a layer of personality that was missing from the collections, as well—of course—as Harrell's explanations that provide further insight."

—David Wills, *Beatdom*

"*A big book, literally and figuratively . . . The Hell's Angels Letters* is a must-have text for any Hunter S. Thompson fan. Lavishly documented and illustrated with the actual correspondence that led to the publication of his breakthrough literary effort . . . The author, Margaret Harrell, who was Thompson's editor on his inaugural book, and her collaborator, Thompson's friend and associate poet Ron Whitehead, have succeeded brilliantly to create a fabulous present for you, or anyone in your life who admires Thompson's numerous achievements . . . It's worth every penny. *The* Hell's Angels *Letters: Hunter S Thompson, Margaret Harrell and the Making of an American Classic* gets five stars out of five! Bravo!"

—Kyle K. Mann, *Gonzo Today*

The *Keep This Quiet!* Series

Keep This Quiet! I: *My Relationship with Hunter S. Thompson, Milton Klonsky, and Jan Mensaert*

"Addictive" and "a delight."

—Mark Strand, U.S. Poet Laureate 1990–'91

"Margaret Harrell's *Keep This Quiet!* offers an illuminating look at Hunter S. Thompson in full throttle trying to make it as a Top Notch prose-stylist. Harrell fills in many important biographical gaps. A welcome addition to what is becoming the HST cottage industry. Read it."

—Douglas Brinkley, editor of *The Proud Highway* and *Fear and Loathing in America*

"Memoir will likely please Hunter S. Thompson fans and appeal to readers with an interest in the beginnings of the post-modern era or the personal sacrifices involved in bringing serious written work to fruition."

—*Kirkus Indie Reviews*

"In the ever-expanding list of biographies and memoirs about Hunter S. Thompson, this latest offering, *Keep This Quiet!* by Margaret A. Harrell, is quite simply a breath of fresh air. . . . What sets *Keep This Quiet!* apart is the extent to which Harrell explores the question of identity and myth, in her quest to simultaneously answer questions concerning her own character and that of one Hunter S. Thompson. As Harrell writes early on—"Who was he? There was no indication how complicated that answer was.""

—Rory Feehan, PhD, owner of https://totallygonzo.org

"Three men, embodiments of three different dimensions of the late 1960's Zeitgeist—wispy dissolution, language-charged intellect, and Gonzo persona-building—are brought together by Harrell to invoke a world of passion and commitment . . . *Keep This Quiet!* is at once noisy, sensual, and word-drunk, as well as quietly intimate and full of Harrell's wonder at her luck. While most readers will come to this book for the Thompson content, in truth all the portraits here—all four of them—are compelling and often touching."

—W. C. Bamberger, *Rain Taxi Review*

"This is no ordinary book about or including Thompson. It's a memoir detailing personal relationships with three authors, the main focus being on Hunter. . . . [I] must stress that this book, as a memoir is quite deep and holds the door open for the reader. While Hunter is a huge selling point, the book has the legs to stand alone."

—Martin Flynn, owner of https://hstbooks.org

Keep THIS Quiet Too! More Adventures with Hunter S. Thompson, Milton Klonsky, Jan Mensaert

"A passionately written memoir that doesn't sit around being fit and proper and straight-laced. If I can use a well-worn phrase here, 'it lifts the lid on so many things.' . . . As a key to the lives of these three writers it is idiosyncratic and in age where blandness is the norm it is a pleasure to go on her journey and find out a little about what made these men tick and what drove her to them."

—*Beat Scene* (UK paper magazine)

Keep This Quiet! III: Initiations

"This is the third and highly recommended title in Margaret Harrell's outstanding *Keep This Quiet!* autobiographical series. A fascinating and very well written personal story, *Keep This Quiet!* III: *Initiations* is very highly recommended for both community and academic library collections. Also exceptionally commended are the first two volumes in this outstanding series, *Keep This Quiet! My Relationship with Hunter S. Thompson, Milton Klonsky, and Jan Mensaert*, and *Keep THIS Quiet Too!*"

—*Midwest Book Review*

Keep This Quiet! IV, rev ed: *Ancient Secrets Revealed*

"As though it arrived with a full legion of angelic messengers and masters of light, from the moment I touched this book, its energy began to flow through me. If you are ready to welcome energetic shifts toward enlightenment, this book is for you. This beautifully written volume of wisdom provides attunements as you meander through its pages joining Margaret on her journey."

—Diana Henderson, author of *Gathering of Angels*
(The Michael Saga)

"Margaret Harrell's blending and merging the whole of a human being and beyond into the cosmos is astounding writing and what a lifetime Journey she has taken to arrive to this book. I feel Margaret is zipping around and catching the flavors of the world, the universe and Beyond. She is working with a whole new and different combined East-West and Middle Paradigm."

—Suzanne V. Brown, PhD, psychologist, former VP, Exceptional Human Experience Network

"Margaret Harrell is a skilled professional writer with excellent ability to communicate and weave esoteric ideas about science, psychology, philosophy, and spirituality. Richard Unger's channeled hand analysis description of her as a 'grand synthesizer' was apt and accurate."

—Ron Rattner, author of the Silly Sutras website and subject, actor in the film *Walks with Ron*, a spiritual memoir.

Also by Margaret A. Harrell
(nonfiction)

Electricity "Transport Trains"
Cloud Conversations & Image Stories
Particle Piñata Poems
The Hell's Angels *Letters: Hunter S. Thompson, Margaret Harrell and the Making of an American Classic*—in collaboration
with Ron Whitehead

Keep This Quiet!
Keep THIS Quiet Too!
Keep This Quiet! III
Keep This Quiet! IV, rev. ed.

Toward a Philosophy of Perception: The Magnitude of Human Potential—Cloud Optics

Marking Time with Faulkner (Literary Criticism)

Space Encounters volumes I–III

Love in Transition volumes I–IV

About the Author

Margaret Ann Harrell was born in North Carolina and educated academically at Duke University (BA, Honors & Distinction in History) and Columbia University (MA in Contemporary British and American Literature). After a brief stint as assistant editor at United Feature Syndicate, Margaret worked as a copyeditor/assistant editor at Random House, New York City, often to first-book writers who later became prominent, such as Hunter S. Thompson. Introduced to parapsychology by J. B. Rhine at Duke University, she eventually found a part of her calling in exploring the meaning and boundaries of consciousness/unconsciousness. She is a three-time fellow at MacDowell Colony.

After thirty adventurous years abroad in Morocco and Europe, in late 2001 she moved back to the United States. Since then, she has been an advanced-meditation light body—luminous-body—teacher in the Orin & DaBen LuminEssence work. Margaret is in demand as a speaker at such events as the Carolina Book and Writer Conference or the Gonzofest in Louisville. Memorably, at the Canessa Gallery in San Francisco in July 2021, she launched *The* Hell's Angels *Letters: Hunter S. Thompson, Margaret Harrell and the Making of an American Classic*, in collaboration with Ron Whitehead, US National Beat Poet Laureate. With expert contributors and reviewers, including the *Washington Post*, this high-end coffee table paperback and limited-edition hard cover is available only at the website of the publisher, Norfolk Press of San Francisco. Earlier, she authored the four-volume memoir series *Keep This Quiet!* (Saeculum University

Press 2011–'18). And before that, in Sibiu, Romania, in English, published the seven-volume nonfiction *Love in Transition* and *Space Encounters* series.

Exhibited in Romania, Italy, Belgium, and New York City in cloud photography, she is fascinated with the sun. Her biography and photography were also many times in Marquis *Who's Who in Modern American Art*. Margaret, a longtime freelance book editor, now edits but not exclusively for authors in the global Self-Publishing School. For a fuller picture, see margaretharrell.com.

Thank You for Reading My Book

Authors live by readers and their reviews. If you enjoyed the poetry
in *Patching Me Together,* I would deeply appreciate an honest
positive review on Amazon and/or other platform. I will read every
word you write and benefit from the comments.
Thank you again and God bless.

www.ingramcontent.com/pod-product-compliance
Lightning Source LLC
Chambersburg PA
CBHW060354130626
46553CB00003B/1233